Our Dark and Radiant Land

Helena Lipstadt

Finishing Line Press
Georgetown, Kentucky

Our Dark and Radiant Land

For my parents
Bala Parzeczewska Lipstadt and David Lipstadt

Copyright © 2023 by Helena Lipstadt
ISBN 979-8-88838-263-9 First Edition

All rights reserved under International and Pan-American Copyright Conventions. No part of this book may be reproduced in any manner whatsoever without written permission from the publisher, except in the case of brief quotations embodied in critical articles and reviews.

Publisher: Leah Huete de Maines
Editor: Christen Kincaid
Author Photo: Isaac Lipstadt
Cover Design: designSimple

Order online: www.finishinglinepress.com
also available on amazon.com

Author inquiries and mail orders:
Finishing Line Press
P. O. Box 1626
Georgetown, Kentucky 40324
U. S. A.

Contents

Preface xi

Que Sera, Sera 1

A Quarrel with the Village of My Birth 7

Necklace 21

Baltic Romance 37

Do Widzenia 59

"Now I Will You to Be a Bold Swimmer" 73

Acknowledgments 78

Poem Index 80

About the Author 83

Preface

It's 2008. I am in my sunny kitchen, half-listening to the radio. I hear two accented voices beginning a conversation. They are an Israeli woman and a Palestinian man. My ears wake up.

Her soldier son had been killed by his soldier son. Hollow with grief, exhausted, lonely, they sought each other out. I marvel at their ability to lay open their pain and hear each other in the midst of their own tragedies.

"Vengeance will never lighten our loss," they say. I imagine the wall between them cracking and crumbling and I realize they have found another way. They have found it, in their agony and anger.

I could, too.

I could begin again.

I could travel to the place where my parents' pasts disappeared, their futures shriveled. I could brave the darkness behind the door.

In May 2011, my nephew, Isaac, and I fly from Los Angeles to Warsaw, Poland. We find lodging in the *Stare Miasto*, the old market square. We come with the bare bones of our story. My mother and father survived the Holocaust together, first in the Warsaw ghetto and then hidden for a year and a half in the cellar of a Polish woman who opened her door when they knocked.

We know that before the war, generations of our family lived in Poland. But that is all we know. Their lives, their stories, were severed by the Holocaust and lost to us.

Until this moment. Neither Isaac nor I have ever stood on Polish ground before. It's not a return, but it feels like a return, the way someone else's memories, repeated again and again, feel familiar.

My parents guarded their stories and I was left to imagine the rest. Now, walking the streets of their cities, I step into the gaps.

I am not prepared for how I feel. This country, which has always represented death to me, is shockingly like home. The smell of lily of the valley. The taste of a pecan cookie. The slide of my palm up a banister. I understand for the first time that exile is not being afloat on a sea, but torn from an actual place, from actual earth.

Isaac and I begin our journey to put flesh on the bones of our Jewish-Polish past. Between 2011 and 2017, I return five more times. I walk the streets of Kalisz and Warsaw, where my parents grew up. I spend days, weeks, a month in Lublin, Szczebrzeszyn, Krakow, Krasnogruda, Łódź and Sejny. Along the way, I encounter open, curious, friendly Poles. Against my early lessons, against my father's admonition to stay away, these people and I become dear friends.

Conversation by conversation, I write a new story for myself about Poland. *My* Poland.

There is another way.

Walk with me.

Que Sera, Sera

Que Sera, Sera

*In Memoriam
William Louis Drazen
1943-1972*

I

What I meant to notice was
your fine hands drumming
on the wheel, the air
like grapes
through Danbury to New Haven.
But we were singing, not
the famous song your uncle
wrote, but *Lay
Lady Lay* and something
from Fairport Convention.
Like every other Friday at 3:00 p.m.
you had taken your Compazine
and we were nearly
to the hospital
with its halo of elms.

II

Long and thin
as a clock hand
ticking twelve
your body lies on our bed.
I place my fingers on your chest,
on the hollow batons
of your ribs.

III

We live north of our fate.
Snow cakes on the porch steps
dense as the air upstairs when I bake
lead bricks and call them bread. Generous,

you eat thin slices with butter and banana.
It is so white in the bedroom,
snowlight cast up from the road.
Your dark brillo hair is live
wires searching for a signal.
We throw your economics
books to the floor. On the cold sheet
we lie together. The melting snow is
my evidence. Once, you and I,
in a sweat of sexlove, here.
I close my mouth now.
I have confessed everything
to you.

IV

Your mother never played
the grand piano in the living room.
But you played
rock and roll radio
and when I called you
on a bet with my friend
Mary Ellen, you knew
Fontella Bass sang *Rescue Me*
in 1965 and how long
she was in the Top 10
and who was #1 before her.
Facts like that,
I could count on. Facts like
when you died
you were 29 years old.
The Harder They Come
by Jimmy Cliff was at the top
of the charts followed
by Neil Young, *Heart of Gold*.
These facts,
they comfort me.

V

We tell no one of your prognosis. Cancer
was contagious then. We don't
even say the word. Not to your best
friend Elliot or your mother or my parents.
While you lie in that floating bed
visiting with ghosts,
I sneak out,
have burning sex
with a Vietnam vet
who knows
about bodies,
and death.

VI

I am on a crowded sidewalk.
I think I am dreaming.
It is Sixth Avenue and
like two vast rivers of fish,
people press urgently
north and south.
After seven years, I see your dark
head above the others. You are
looking down, but steady move
toward me. I am helpless
with hope. You come close.
If I could lift my hand, I would
open my palm on the long
plane of your chest.
Very slow, you raise your head.
You look into my eyes.
Your eyes are brown,
as always.
Like rain you speak to me.
"I will meet you,"
you say, "in the Andes."
Then you disappear.

A Quarrel With the Village of My Birth

A Quarrel With the Village of My Birth

which is not a village but
a shivering capital
of Europe, may she rot and be
reborn with heart. Even her
birthday song is martial. Even
her avenues are lined with
pikes. Even her galleries
crowded on Sunday, her parks
larded with pigeons and crumbs.
Marlena, husky voice and
droop lid, sits on my lap in
promiscuous lush. Of course
I am charmed and reach for wine.
Of course it spills red across
the continent of my table.
Like an orphan I want you.

All That I Have Is a River

Who were you, and how did you get here? How long are you able to stay? Did you walk, did you ride, were you carried?

Did Prince Bolesław allow you to live here, did he sign a legal decree? Did he sign it in Kalisz in 1264? Did your neighbors brush by you, not looking?

Your mother gave you what love-name? In the courtyard did your sisters fight? Did your father lay his hand on your shoulder, did he brush back dark hair from your face?

Who sewed your pants pocket, what coins did you carry? If you brought enough coins, if you did enough business, if you kept yourself out of the way.

Did you quarrel with your neighbor, what name did he call you? How high did you climb in his oak tree? Did you gather up acorns to throw?

Were your shoes made of leather? Did you have a fine dress or only the one? Was your house made of brick, of wood, or stone? Was your roof made of thatch? Did rain drip in, was it smoky in winter, and dark?

Did you each have a bedroom or share where you slept? Did you hear each other snore, weep, make love?

Did King Kazimierz the Great re-sign the Statute? Was his invitation to witness politely accepted? Did your neighbor come over, stand with you in your doorway saying *moje gratulacje* and you מזל טוב-ed him back?

Did you bring back their brown goose that escaped to your yard, did they bring you red cabbage, white cheese?

Did you roll out thin pastry for strudel? Did you fill it with cherries and walnuts? Did you deliver a plate to your neighbor, and place it in her two hands?

At the wedding, did you play *Di Mezinke Oysgegebn* on your mandolin? Did you all raise a glass? Did the father salute you with plum wine, did you call it slivowitz or schnapps?

Did you stand at your fence, lean across to inquire on the health of her mother today? Did you hand her a bottle of elixir to use for that cough? Did she blame you when her mother got sicker?

Did you meet your betrothed on a Shabbos? Had you known his family for years, did you play together as children? Was there love before duty in your marriage? How many children survived?

Did you have a small store or a booth in the guildhall? How did you learn to work silver? From your father, his father, his father before? Did you filigree silver like lace? Did you tuck gemstones into your linings?

Who sewed your pants pocket, what coins did you carry? If you brought enough coins, if you did enough business, if you kept yourself out of the way.

Did you have a small boat built of ash, did you haul it down the bank of the Warta and throw in a line to catch sturgeon? The fatter the better, in fish.

All that you had was a river, guard to your watery peace, your quiet float in the morning, and sentinel of your escape. You called it the Warta in Sieradz, the Prosna in Kalisz, the Wisła in Warszawa, and the Oder that flows to Berlin

where I met you, sliding through borders, Poland to Germany, mother to daughter, carrying your mysteries, your comings and goings, and the river sustains us without even trying.

Do Widzenia, 1

Warsaw 1941 my parents meet in the only place two young Jews can meet: the Ghetto. She fled from the old city of Kalisz to the west. He is from Warsaw, its gritty neighborhood of Praga. With the passion of wartime, they fall in love. They survive together in a cellar hiding place. After the Soviet Army liberates Poland from the East, they go West. They smuggle out of Poland in a coal barge on the Oder River to Berlin. Hidden under the coal, my mother is pregnant with me.

They leave behind her father's grave in the Jewish cemetery. All the rest is rubble. They never return.

My mother was from the rolling rich land of southwest Poland, of Sieradz and Kalisz, where storks nest on the chimney tops and sour pickles are set out in a crock on the breakfast buffet. She was the youngest of four, brother Moishe, Mala the hero, unknowable Esterka and then Bala, born 1919.

When my father, David, was a boy, he learned Torah and Talmud dawn to dusk at a Warsaw *cheder* down the block. He lived with his mother, his father, his two sisters, Fela the elder, and sweet Lilka. He and his father listened to *Aida* from the balcony of the Grand Theatre, and whistled arias on the tram ride home.

Then War.

It becomes unthinkable to love the place that once nurtured them. Now we are all cut off from that place. None of us can love it.

Half-light

Four hundred kilometers we drove under
May's lacework and it was fox dark
and deer leap from Warsaw.
Lakes lay back on the rise
and fall of hillbreath.

Crumbs the crows have not yet swallowed
crumbs my mother let fall
as she looked the other way.
My Poland. I'm looking at you.

Bala from Kalisz, Air, Earth

1.
In a triangle
of clean white cloth
you swing like a pendulum
from the stork's beak.

Your untried feet dangle,
the stork's wings beat
you stare into her chest
she carries you

from a place
you don't remember
to a place
you can't imagine,
the grit you will need
today,
      (pulse)
today,
      (pulse)
every,
      (pulse)
day.

2.
On hands and knees
you and the *rolnik*
hunt for mushrooms.

He carries a willow basket,
a jar of water, a cloth for wiping
the clinging loam.

The *rolnik* holds out his hand.
In his skin you feel
his dry crust and sour soup.

documents of flight

when the knock comes on the door
        what do we take with us?

do we carry everything in one suitcase?
        are we walking are we running?

            and when we arrive, far away
white cedar, where we are going,

      how will we prove we were once
born, linden, in the place that is no more,

           married there, owned that wooden house,
had these children, died?

and if we want to return someday, linden,
        to that place we left,

will the authorities
            who red-stamped the documents

    we no longer have
               let us in?

Names Go Traveling With No Valises

My mother's names:
Bala Basia Bayla Barbara

My father called her Bala?
with a questioning lilt
as if afraid he'd lost her,
which is how I know her,
two soft syllables, sometimes made softer,
Basia, and I melt,
a child in love with my mother,
and also afraid
I'll lose her.
In disguise, her false identity
card stamped "Barbara,"
strangely English and foreign, but there
in black and white is her young face.

My father's names:
David Dovid'l Tadzik Tadeusz

She called him *Tadzik,*
without fear, until the end
when everything splintered
and she searched for him desperate
if he stepped out of sight.
But in Yiddish he was *Dovid'l,*
a young man again with a harp
and beloved.

These are the names of his parents:
Hentsche and *Hirschel* from Warszawa.
These are the names of her parents:
Adele and *Aron Ber* from Sieradz.

They board the train,
they disembark,
they start over.

Lichen

1.
On Yom Kippur the rabbi
drags a damp rock into the hall
this is your cemetery she says
place your pebbles here

nameless all my relations crowd me
they swarm my chest   release themselves
out of my eyes   I let go

2.
Your trail is cold.
I hunt
for letters
long rubbed away or stolen
from one century to another

lichen drills
into the walls of your grave
its fingers creep
break the bones of your shelter

I look for you in the last place your name was laid
look for you where your daughter
dropped leaves of prayer on your bed of
rest and unrest

3.
I look for you in the dark   tap on trunks
wait for gleam of rain to shine
on one *Alef* one *Resh*

I lap water
from your headstone
swallow and discharge into air

your name   Aron-Ber   אהרן בער

Playing Piano Between Wars

All it takes
is a tango.
I play for her
        and she steps out.

A hungry woman
deckle edged, her slide
of cheek turned away.
        I look for her asleep,

awake, in concert halls,
tea rooms, in hotels.
So many lovely chances.
        I hide behind

the black piano, offer golden scales
for her to climb from where
brother death has laid her.
        Come, Mala, bring

your sister of no grave, your mother, lost.
Night after night I play for you,
conjure you,
        tango

Like a Badger

       Like a badger

              chased

                        by
                            d a c h s h u n d s
     I keep
   r e a c h i n g

for a
    burrow
        to
                this language
    of
ours
    mama

underground

Necklace

Necklace

My name hangs
like a pendant
in the necklace of generations.
Link after link of *h* & *n*
Hannah is Hebrew for Grace
threaded through Slavic cities
washed new in the *mikveh*
to shine, a red squall between
my mother's legs.

A name is heavy to carry
down the wide hopeful avenue
and light, after so many repetitions
so many prayers.

It dodges the fluid borders
of seven countries
collects the patina of a Polish song.
"The Lovely Helena"
whistled on the corner
hands in pockets
in dangerous times
a hiding place
of a name.

Burn a hole in the map of Warsaw
look through the ash circle
you can't see
the flamed soul of Hannah
my grandmother wearing
her grandmother's name
singing mine to me.
Every day I cast off her hungry voice
bear my light a blaze
in the eye.
A name is heavy to carry
and light.

Speaking to the Dead

You stand over and below me   I inhale the shimmer
of your breath   Let me not be thief of your story
I will not betray your blame

Perhaps you are resting and I disturb   perhaps
you are where I put my father   wise and full
of sympathy   now that he has crossed over
sees how small we are   how full of longing

I will not betray your blame   the dead
need their space   mothers and fathers
of my liquid core   I pull you from the acid

burying ground of my mind   and plant you
my eyes sluice water   to feed you
where can I bend   *gdzie?*   where can I kneel   *gdzie?*
where can I place   this food of stones?

Everybody Knows

Like a fisherman I cast
my nets over the crowd
in the station.

Again I look for my
cousin who was never born.
All the doors of a dark

hallway burst
open at the light in her eyes.
In our journey we climb

over many chairs. I taste
their brittle backs.
Through the window I see

a false baroness lean
into a green velvet chair,
dress her long Polish hair

with the silver-handled
brush we left behind.
No matter, our hips knock

against a new land,
green as a robin's
nest. Years gone, my

mother and father sit
above me,
shoulders, knees.

They save my seat and tell
the story everybody
knows, of the dark,

the coal barge.

Snake I Come

Sidewinder   all muscle and grit   wrap myself around and squeeze   kiss I do mouth all over   I would swallow you   so furious   squeeze I do   harder   harder

You don't know with what fury I would love you   a history of fury   a war of it I hold your breasts in my hands   my mouth makes wet trails over them cutting and burning   milking   nourish me

I will leave no history   no criss-cross thread   trails of piss   no iron nails   pages torn   no memory of my rout across your body   all the while I will look you in the eye   snake of love   fasten you to me because we both know

a cutting light runs like a blade between us and you say no   I am afraid   what else could lead me to you so strong but the dazzling light of death   the feathered bird   Poland's shield   snake in her claws   lifting from the fire

The hottest love brings together your cunt and my fist   and you want my fist in your cunt   to be filled and torn apart   have me slither in   own   conquer   turn you inside out   molting and pregnant

Cry I cry   underground   deep dripping I cry   shaggy and rocking   dark I squeeze   in and in   tighter   smaller   carbon in a cave

Squeeze I squeeze   my eyes have never opened   my transparent fingers scratch your skin   you bleed just a little   forgive me   I am always newborn and pliant   you overlook the iron nails dragging   the rusty nails left so long in the rain of that mildewed continent   I tie you up with tears   my useless weapon

I want to nail my fangs into you   love you so hard   you die   have you survive to love again   we must both survive   I look into your open eyes while I touch you   my fingers and tongue raise fiery welts   you flood   how much is fear   how much desire

Burned to ash   I hide in the chamber   empty and ruined   fury pulls out like a rip tide   my muscles slacken   the hollow tubes of my teeth empty poison I can no longer contain   I imitate death   silent and still

Between the dead and the dangerous   I love the danger   turn me inside out   snake slithers out   snake needs to feed   my mouth is wide open   jaw unhinged   hypnotize then gorge and ruminate long   fanged and venomous   glittering and gorgeous   love you to death.

each field has its blooms
blood red poppy in the wheat
one drop, one soldier

Do Widzenia, 2

Until I went there, I didn't know how much of Poland they had clinging to their skin. How much of it my mother put on the table in the soup bowl, my father put in his heated curses, how much in the cantorial music he loved, her Chopin.

She is gone now twenty years. I can't remember her voice. I can't summon any of my senses to hold her here, not sound, not smell, not touch. I step into a Warsaw pastry shop and look through the glass between me and the trays of cookies and see my mother's cookies, the crescent-shaped butter cookies I rolled between my palms in our kitchen and placed on the baking sheet in a row next to hers. And I wonder: is this place mine? This reviled, cursed place?

I travel to Poland with Isaac, my nephew. We go to Kalisz, where my mother was from. We go to Warsaw, where my father was born, we stand on busy Targowa Street, stare at the three-story building in which my father had been a child, stare and stare, waiting for him to come out.

Near the Prosna River in Kalisz I find the old Jewish cemetery. The old cemetery is from the 1200s, nearly a thousand years ago.

The Scarecrow

She is planted knee deep in the garden
wearing a dress of faded rose
her arms outflung in welcome.

Each stub swings a lantern
candled with the flame
of every crossroad shrine

adorned for special prayers
in May, Mary's month
fresh plastic flowers

spill out devotion once danced
in groves of oak
under a nimbus moon.

If fate has brought you here,
read the sign of the crossroads,
where you kneel not knowing,

every way shrouded
and the sharp beaks of crows.

Doina in the Study House

You remember surely
this is history she said
the history of leaving
and returning she said.
Notes were cut off, halls
shrouded, stones baffled.
I do not make this up
the thick stones of Sejny
yeshiva hold a clear
cadence echo seven
generations of pages
turning, chant repeating,
from Vilna, Jerusalem
of the North, a scant leap
away. When I put ear
to stone I hear as do
Wojciech and Michał
who put lip to trumpet
rehearse their Klezmer
Orkestr here blow out
the very *nigun* of
yeshiva boys who learned
pages of Talmud in
these halls. If you are a
musikant or an
historian and put
ear to stone you hear
and the need to play
that thunderous tune grips.
You hear history on your back,
the weight of it, creak open.

Imagine the Snail

Like the marks of a fork, the dirt road
scratches through Polish fields
fresh and green with wheat.

She pulls a stalk.
How one part fits into the other,
an elegant pen in its cap.

The wheat is tender, full of juice
like the snail by her feet
with its ice-thin house on its back,
its slick ride of muscle.

She kneels down to see the snail
when frames of an old film
begin to unwind in the tree line,
in bitter acres of beeches behind,
where native foreigners once hid
and after a winter of twigs and frozen roots
devoured stalks, frogs, snails,
a spring feast of gristle and bark.

Slow she stands, looks beyond
field and quiet farmhouse
where clouds pile gray with rain.

White stork flaps above,
ra-ratchet of car out of sight,
mosquito bleeds her neck.

She rattles the edges of the film, spools it
tight in its compact case, snaps it shut,
back to the middle of a green, green field,
this wheat only wheat, this snail only snail.

In the Upstairs Bedroom

Polish words stumble up the stairs
like animals their hair
and hot red breath. Cat quiet
words wrap around her ankles,
trip her into believing she understands.

And she does, she understands
that she is standing on a step,
that she is meeting someone
she has never met before
but knows, like the skinwarm scent
of her mother's bedclothes.

Twaróg

All I can do is point.
I can't speak to the clerk,
or read out the label
only point to the wedge,
white as milk
lying in the cold case.

The lettering on the wrapper
is red and blue,
the paper damp.
The clerk swaddles the cheese
then tucks each end well under.

Now it lies on the kitchen counter
the curds cross-hatched
with the pattern of cloth
from which it hung to drain.

I cut a red apple into quarters
place them on a dish and lay
the soft cheese to one side.

I pick up a morsel of cheese
between thumb and finger
open my mouth, and there

stands my father
seven years dead
reaching for a piece of *twaróg*
with thumb and finger.

I sit, I stand,
walk out of the room
walk back,
he is here,
clear and about to eat
serem bialem,
farmer's cheese,
in a place
he fled forever.

Not Asking

I never asked you,
what was your father like?

was it because
> you cried alone in your bedroom
> behind the thin door

because
> you flew apart sometimes, tectonic,
> and I was scared

because
> you were keeping me from some truth,
> that I didn't really want to know

because
> you were a mystery I couldn't solve and one more
> would be too many

because you
> were protecting me and I was protecting you

because

because

Baltic Romance

Baltic Romance

I seem to be at sea without a compass
Scanning the shores for sunken trunks of gold
The Baltic ice obscures the city's entrance
The gates hold back the rush of beggar's cold

I cannot hear the music of your amber
I dare not meet the man who takes the toll
The only sound is beating on the tambour
The only sound the moon flight of the owl

When will we land in waters safe and shallow
Where will we find the story we were told
How will we know which byway we should follow
Which sign to read, which hand to hold?

It Could Happen

Just like that
in front of a hotel
in a world capital
two women in dark glasses
walk by
while I am distracted

by the way the cedar grows
above the parapet
distracted from
my magpie search
of crowded plazas
lunchtime sidewalks

for someone of certain age
or slope of cheek
a tossed-up shard
of scattered family
long fled
to smoking railways.

(Step, pause, the younger
lowers her glasses,
it could happen,
she lowers
her glasses,
she stutters
my name.)

Travel to Szczebrzeszyn

Not far from the Carpathians, to Szczebrzeszyn,
on the west bank of the Wieprz.
Travel by cart on top of the hay. The horse pulls,
her head down.
Climb from the cart to the steps of the new synagogue
painted impossible pink.

Make a circle with artists and students,
turn to re-making something that was
a 17th-century world, when townsfolk in provinces
had respite from warring
when a synagogue like this stood
in an eastern town square
dark wood on the outside painted Eden within.

Here I paint flowers on a pale blue ceiling
once covered with flowers in hundreds,
carmine, lampblack, chalk.
Here I am part of a reach back into history
building a new version of an old synagogue
with zodiacal creatures,
two-headed eagles, six-tailed fish,
an encircling ribbon of psalms in black Hebrew script.

I crush powder for hours mulling grains of pigment
to make paint, woad blue.
Like a pilgrim I know nothing
except in my shoulders my hips why I am pushing
past teatime past dinner to finish the petals
on one of my flowers when never before
have I painted like this.

Like this, in Poland, like this in a synagogue
like this in my belly of knots.

Like this, when Agata working beside me,
tells of her grandfather crying over his vodka
never knowing why until she grew older
and asked him about life before war.

Like this when Agata shivers. What life was like, before?

My belly and eyes start to brim over while guiding
the muller in tight figure-eights.
Go on, Agata, tell me, more. And she asks me what, and I ask her why
and we both stop and see the sky changing to night.

This is the moment, this very moment, colliding
with blue-eyed Agata, my enemy, my murderer.
Shake me, Poland, you can. Here I am pulsing
on a bridge of flowers in pigment
and you still grow poppies out of your earth
like you grew my family generations before.

I keep returning, boarding five airplanes keep flying into your cities
listening to Chopin on Sunday in the park
listening to Krzysztof, to Joasia, to Agata,
meeting a me that never left here
some lyric some piece of breath that fell on that linden
that blossoms in summer that bees make into honey
that I stir into tea and drink while it's hot.

Do Widzenia, 3

Time after time in my life there are departures. Always there is good reason for me to move to another town. Full of hope and slivers of regret, I leave. I leave the long winters of New England, the progressives of Philadelphia. I leave lovers, land, work.   Goodbye.

I don't really know about being from someplace. I am from my parents, and they were from Hell.

Native Speaker

Everyone, on some mornings,
wants to lose herself.

The fog is perfect thick.
I push the boat out
into the water
of this north Atlantic cove,
no passport to the country I want
with its dock on the Baltic Sea.
My paddle thunks against the gunwale.

A young girl asks, "Where are you from?"
I do not give my usual answer
in three languages
because my ears
are full of Szczebrzeszyn
and I cannot paddle this canoe
across the sea.

But I want to be close
to my mother and my father
this morning, wherever they are.
I reach into the undivided fog,
gather threads of sound,
knit together a sail of language,
full of mist, full of holes.

Like One of Those

At the Archive I float,
a long table,
six scratched
leather-bound books.

I tilt open pages
big as platters
my pointer finger slow dragging
over name, name, name.

Once, they lived here,
by the slow-moving Warta River
by apples fallen
ripe to ground.

Arm-in-arm in heavy coats
they *spaziered*
across the square
in 1845 and 1855 and 1865.

They did exist
because I see their names
fine long strokes
on heavy paper

with edges still sharp
and an extra skin
of dust.
I rub the skin

with my finger
bring it to my lips.
It smells of spiders.

Deliverance

This morning by the lake in Krasnogruda
I am mute.

Consonants push at my palate, scrape at my ears
float past, cunning as fish.

> *Toe deep at the barefoot shore*
> *a curly child*
> *learns the world*
> *by setting tongue*
> *against teeth*
> *nh-nh.*

I contrived my own hostage at this lakeside
in boats lined
with poems
only I hear.

Climbing on the splintery dock
I spread my arms east and west
lean back my head, offer up
my parched my
blue veined
throat
nh-nh.

gray wind off the lake
in the forest hide the birds
what ears catch their song?

In Krasnogruda the Cuckoo Wakes Me

Rain heavy air spools
around my boots
I walk out
smell the early lilacs
see the gardener
in the yard.

I arrange my mouth
for greeting *Dzien dobry*
and he lifts
his pale blunt face.

Like a nestling
he bends his head,
takes my hand and kisses it
touches his forehead
and waits.

As if I, a Jew, am not
like him with skittish heart
pulsing under down.

As if I had stepped
out of a Manor house
in the Grand Duchy of Lithuania
and had power
over his brown bread.

Transgress

I look behind the door again
I am a guest here in Kraków

and have provoked an invitation
dependent on charm

I think I know
the hard bricks of the courtyard

outside, how wet they are, red, cold
and am determined to remain

at the table, the cloth draped
whitely over my knees.

All the while I am scorchingly
aware of your sufferance.

Neither of us knows
where this meeting will lead

too much is hidden
showing desire is a crime

and my excessive appetite
for utopia keeps surfacing

like a big-mouthed fish.
I pretend

I am satisfied
with what has fallen

slickly on my plate
but you hear me whisper,

more.

Do Widzenia, 4

Something is happening to me in Warsaw. It is happening in my ears. I follow people down the sidewalk to hear them speak Polish. It has been so many years since I heard my parents speak it that I forget I understand. My senses call out. The connection resides in the clay of me, in the music of me.

At the corner of Swietojanska and the Rynek, *babushka*-ed women sit on low stools selling bouquets of lily of the valley from overflowing buckets. I buy three bouquets and fill our hotel room with perfume. I am wild for Chopin. I swoon over borscht. Isaac and I drink Żubrówka vodka. I am drunk on this place.

Like a hangover, images of war intrude. It plays back and forth this way.

The soft parts all rubbed away

You run your palm up and down the wooden
doorframe. I follow you, pause my fingers

at each nick and splinter.
We cock our heads like doctors listening for a cough

tap on the doorframe tease out shapes
where the *mezuzah* might have lived.

Somewhere in this building
my father was a kid with two parents,

two sisters. He chased Lilka in the yard
raced Fela up the stairs, unlocked one of these doors.

You help me seek and speak, you know this land
its language and its long-ago.

What is left
a burnished handrail, cobbles in the courtyard.

The soft parts all rubbed away
our fingers coarse from foraging.

Tante Fela

I am not as tall as I was
when I looked like Polly Bergen
and strolled down the shady
Warsaw sidewalk a leather bag
in the crook of my arm.
Today in Bnei Brak I am bent
like a Palestine sunflower
picked over by crows.

In the courtyard below, the clatter
of quick feet on stone. The *Hasidim*
to their morning prayers,
me to mine in the kitchen.
I stretch these knuckled fingers for my coffee
and find a ghost battering out of the steam.

I still have the skirt pushed
to the back of my closet,
pleats like knives.
Like a locust in stubble
after the hay is cut
I have made my peace.

But the blowing sand talks to me
of such long loneliness
I sometimes look for
what is no longer here,
a man in a gray suit
with his hat
tilted over
his eyes.

First Person Singular

Before you come to Poland
leave your pronouns in a jar.

You won't use them here
in the center of Europe,

unbuckled from your
new world straining

for fifteen famous minutes
and your panoply of skins.

You'll find a buttery homogeneous melting
of common kitchens, common tongues

into flock, fold, and chorus
so when you want to say, *I'm coming,*

just say, *Coming.*
They'll know who you are.

Kitchen

When there
are as many
languages
in a kitchen
as chairs
around the table
the child eats
them all
and is easy
with
polyphony.

She may
become
a chef
of linguistic
proportion
the rest of her
life
slicing
strudel from
kielbasa
chlodnik from
cholent
and inventing
momentous
recombinations
called
Soup

W kuchni

"Kitchen" translated into Polish by Zdzisław Dudek

w której więcej języków niż stołów
dziecko pochłania je wszystkie
bawiąc się
polifonią

Może kiedyś wymyśli nowe dania
niczym językoznawca
do końca życia definiując
różnicę pomiędzy
czulentem a struclą
humusem a kiełbasą
i dokonując wiekopomnego
wynalazku pomieszania
zwanego
Zupą

New Content

The grass is sunwarm and green.
It is spring in Krasnogruda.
I am lying on a bed of earthworms.
I don't hear them, I don't smell them,

I don't care that they're working
their horizontal way
to the big red door
of the Manor House.

Milosz's ghost lingers in the eaves.
I didn't come here to meet
a Serbian blonde.
I came to unbury

Poles, preferably
from Warsaw,
preferably long lost.
Ksenija teaches me to say,

"Hello friend"
in Polish, then
in Serbian, for luck.
She leads me

from the library
to the dock.
She lays her hand
on my shoulder

names six kinds
of shorebirds
that nest
on Holny Lake

pulls back
the reeds
nods to where
otters slide
slick, into the water.

fringe the lake in reeds
in the forest hide the birds
what ears catch their song?

Do Widzenia

Do Widzenia, 5

Here in Poland, I carry my mother with me. Just by being here I tear open her carefully sealed heart.

My father articulated a clear injunction: Don't go to Poland. Yet when I stroll through Lazienki Park, and sit down on a bench under a towering Catalpa tree, it comes to me that I must tell my father I am here. He is so alive in me at that moment I don't remember he is five years gone.

He said don't go. His blood-saturated admonition held sway for many years, but enough time has passed for one generation to die and a new one to be born. I am the life between the two, and I am here, ready to turn my face, the way a sunflower does. I am ready to let go of an old story of pain without end and enemies without redemption.

This summer again I travel to Poland. I walk again in Warszawa, on a grassy verge above the Wisla River. I listen to the shshsh syllables of Polish.

My ears lust after the sound. I return to the bakery to see if they are still making my mother's cookies. They are.

Many ghosts live in this great city, Warszawa. For a thousand years, Jews lived in Poland, trading goods with the townsfolk in the market square, building synagogues next door to churches, swapping melodies with the Poles. There is no Polish history without Jews. Like sensing an amputated limb, Poles feel something missing.

I know something is missing. The story of my family has been the story of war and exile. Our history wraps me in a shawl of smoke.

I imagine stepping into a new story, one where I let the sibilant syllables twine, paint the flowers of an old *shul* on new walls, claim this place where surely one of my family has planted seeds and harvested. Peeling back through pain I open myself to this land, to this people, build a raft and pole across.

All by myself

All by myself,
I am having an affair
with you

you don't care
you don't know
że Cię kocham

I'm wrapping
my lips
around you

your tongue
your throat
your body of cherries

your smell, familiar
as an orchard
of dangling fruit, fallen,

then folded in a cone of paper
I don't want to be rid
of you, I can't

it would be like tearing
the pink belly from my peonies,
the bark off my tree.

Spring Ice

❧

In early spring when the ground begins to thaw, shallow puddles form in low places on the road. Snow lingers under the trees and the woodcock flutters high above the field. At night, the frost comes back. It forms a skin over the puddles, translucent, and just strong enough to lure one to step, tentative, onto the ice, and hope it will hold.

❧

Sometimes I play the 'what if' game. What if my parents had not fled Poland after the war? What if they had felt Jewish *and* Polish? Staying or going might look like a choice from here, but for them to stay, in burned and cratered Poland, would have meant they felt a depth of rootedness and carried a vision of healing I can't imagine.

Perhaps they felt there was no choice. Perhaps what they lost and what they feared was all they saw of Poland. Perhaps they asked each other, "Does it matter if we leave this slant of light, this river?" Perhaps the shining light of somewhere else was good medicine. On my dark mornings in the long nights of winter, their ability to go forward at all is beyond me.

My mother was pregnant with me in 1946 when my parents smuggled out of Poland hidden on a river barge under a pile of coal. My mother's anguish, which I absorbed through our blood, was unfiltered. She protected me as she could, with her body. Because I was formed in and of her, I ask these questions. Of course, I wish I could ask my parents about this, and so many other things, but somewhere in me, I feel that my asking is also their asking, is my pull to Poland, the other road.

I try on "choice," wear their decisions as garments I can put on and take off, free and not free to imagine myself as a Jewish-Polish girl in Warsaw. I collage these options together. There are shadows and light in this game. My parents were brave in either version, stay or go. They were ferocious enough to imagine crossing the abyss and starting again.

❧

I ask now, "what if." What if I had been born there?
The world I see is Poland, my first river, the Wisla, flowing north to the Baltic

Sea. My first language is Polish. I learn early to twist my tongue over tangled k's and z's.

I know Kalisz, where my mother grew up. I walk through the leafy quadrants of Park Miejski to the Prosna river, watch rowers in skiffs on bright water. In September we take our baskets to the forest and gather mushrooms.

I know Sieradz, where my grandfather was born, where he walked in the winter, shawled and hatted, on the frozen road along the Warta river. In summer, he picked blackberries by the Warta, and so do I.

east sun on my cheek
dirt road stretches through birches
where may you find me

৺
We are Jewish, my parents said, not Polish. Don't go to Poland.

I fly from Los Angeles to Poland, travel through the country by bus, train and car and meet Poles, mostly young and Catholic. A handful are Jews.

With a few, a frisson of recognition. Something to explore, some affinity or attraction.   All the mysteries apply.

Why are these meetings miraculous to me? Because my very existence feels like a miracle and so does theirs, given war, given chance? Because traveling to Poland at all was so unlikely? Because finding common ground with Poles is unmapped territory? My early lessons slammed those doors shut.

But here I am, enamoured (trying to be, wanting to be) with these curious Poles. Bit by bit we talk, share food, laugh, my old story (enemy, enemy) begins to drain away.

My relations with these Poles is not easy. We learn to navigate the open and closed places between us. I am their Jew and they are my Poles.

The Polish language itself is a barbed fence, one I have climbed since I was a child, one I learned to decipher young but never to speak out loud. It catches and cuts me, trips me. I'll never understand, never speak.

My Poles and I are weighted with our past and our future. How far can we go? How deep? When will we come to unclimbable walls, buried antipathy? Will we climb, will we unbury?

Krzysztof, Joasia, Agnieszka.

If I had grown up in Poland, I might not have started a conversation with Krzysztof on the bus. He would simply be a young man who sat beside me on a seven-hour ride from Vilnius to Warsaw. Or opened myself to Joasia, who took me under her wing for a month in the northeast village of Krasnogruda. Or discovered Agnieszka, whose father read her Sholom Aleichem stories at bedtime and she woke up dreaming of Yiddishland.

❦
Agnieszka in Los Angeles.

Agnieszka and I meet in Los Angeles after a lecture she gives on post-war Poland. A direct gaze, a red-lipped smile, Agnieszka is warm and curious, a Yiddish scholar, but not Jewish. We hit it off instantly.

When we meet the next day for coffee, Agnieszka says she is interviewing Los Angeles Jews about their connection to Yiddish culture. She asks spontaneously, "May I interview you?"

That evening she comes to my house, videographer and equipment in tow, and for an hour and a half she asks about my background. I pour out stories that usually lay on a back shelf. I even find myself singing—in Yiddish—a wry song my father made up about a Warsaw Jew raising chickens on a farm in Connecticut.

On a fine day the following May, we meet again, in Kraków. Agnieszka has offered to drive me the length of Poland in her tiny Fiat, north from Kraków to the rolling hills near Sejny. We have ten hours in the car and an overnight at her mother's house in Gizycko, in the lake district.

Our talk sashays, Yiddish, English and back. We get out of the car often to admire the dozens of roadside shrines to Mother Mary, lavishly decorated with spring flowers, lily of the valley, tulips, and loops of ribbon in yellow and red. Back in the car, our dialogue is easy and far ranging until she asks, "Did your parents own property in Poland before the war?" To escape where I fear this might be going, I quickly say, "I don't know." And let it drop.

Joasia in Suwalszczyzna

In Sejny, I meet twenty-eight-year-old Joasia, cultural worker at Borderland Foundation. I am writer-in-residence for the month of May and she is my liaison. We spend long laughing afternoons by Holny Lake as she tries to push Polish into my stubborn head.

Joasia takes her pedagogy seriously. She makes charts and devises word games.

I am afraid I disappoint her, but in one early success she teaches me to say to the neighboring farmer, *"Chciałbym kupić dwanaście yayka,"* "I would like to buy a dozen eggs."

One afternoon we swim far out into the lake. Halfway across we pause and float, moving our arms and legs just enough to keep our heads above water. "Have you ever known a Jew before?" She thinks for a moment. "No."

Otters slide through the lake-edge reeds, their heads pop out of the water. I turn to look at the surround of spring green hills. Just last month, Joasia tells me, the fields were still covered in snow and the edges of the lake hid thin shelves of ice. I turn on my back and squint up to the brilliant sky.

In what moment besides this one, could Joasia and I have become friends? In what moment besides this one could she and I have gathered wild strawberries, taken Rumi the dog for a long walk past the farms?

Three years later, Joasia and I meet in Warsaw for a day. Eager, I wait for her bus at the Central Bus Station. We walk to a nearby outdoor café and for three hours, catch up.

When we stand to stretch, Joasia suggests the National Gallery on Jerozolimskie Street. Inside, she has the ease of an educated native, pulling me behind her from room to room. We step into a vast hall with twenty-foot-wide paintings. I watch her as she tells me about the work. Her head and shoulders tilt forward, almost falling into the oiled layers of Jan Matejko's enormous, volcanic painting, into the horrified ecstasies of trampled peasants, the loft of heaven rising on clouds. Joasia's blond hair is pulled back into a tail, high and arched like the tail of the hero's white horse in *The Battle of Grunwald*.

Afterward, we walk up Krakowskie Przedmiescie to a traditional restaurant for *fuczki*, sauerkraut pancakes and *kvass*, a surprising drink of fermented rye. Joasia is always putting new Polish sweets and savories on my plate. My mouth remembers every bite, every sip.

Krzysztof in Lublin

I settle into my seat for the seven-hour bus ride from Vilnius, Lithuania to Warsaw, my eyes still full of Anna Karenina, the ballet I saw last night at the National Drama Theater. Even though I hitch up my shoulder and turn my face to the window, young, bespectacled Krzysztof sits down next to me. Polite, at first, we exchange names, then somehow fall headlong into family stories, his grandfather, my parents, stories that spill out until dusk, when the bus pulls in to the Central Bus Station in Warsaw. I don't remember ever saying I'm a Jew.

We keep in touch between Warsaw and Los Angeles. Three years later, we meet again in Warsaw in Łazienki Park. "I have an idea," Krzysztof tells me under the catalpa trees. "I would like to invite you to visit my city, Lublin."

"Yes!"

The next year, Krzysztof arranges everything. We stay with his welcoming parents in their Lublin apartment. He organizes a three-day tour of vanished Jewish Lublin.

A cold drizzly October day. Krzysztof, his wife, Maria, and I walk through the Old City, where Jews lived before the war. We climb dark stairs inside the original city gates, *Brama Grodzka*, the passage from Christian to Jewish Lublin, once a meeting place of traditions and religions. What used to be the Jewish Quarter is now a huge parking lot.

Brama Grodzka holds "Memory of a Place" a photo-documentary exhibit with scrupulous detail of the Jewish community: which Lublin streets they lived on, who was in the family, their work. And here is Krzysztof, reading each snippet about people he knew nothing of.

Later we walk through town, up a steep hill to the cemetery, wait to meet the man with the key who will unlock the iron gate for us. We slip and slide over wet grass, squint out names on granite, Shalom Shakna ben Yosef and Moshe Isserles, illustrious rabbis who taught and prayed in Lublin five hundred years ago.

Krzysztof's attention is clinched. "I never really knew my city. So many Jews lived here! And Lublin, vital in the Jewish world." He turns to face me. "I'm so angry! The Soviets kept our history from us. Lublin is my place, my city, and I thought I knew her, but I didn't. Not any of this."

I listen to Krzysztof with two hearts. One heart staggers under the weight of gravestones. One heart is with him, full of anger about the Soviet times and Lublin's erased Jews. While part of me embraces him, another part feels very Jewish and alone.

That evening, back at Krzysztof's parents' apartment, we eat as much as we can hold of the feast his mother, Danuta, set out for us: hot cabbage borscht served in a cup, two kinds of fried fish, one called "Greek" fish, cooked in tomatoes, mushrooms-and-onions, (Krzysztof laughingly admits he has no idea why it was called "Greek" since it was clearly a Polish dish), sliced tomatoes with minced sweet onion, a platter of yellow cheeses, herring and onions, fresh rolls filled with mushrooms, four types of bread and butter, hard-cooked eggs with mayonnaise-and-chive dressing, a platter of sliced fresh white cheese, cherry wine homemade by Danuta, then homemade cherry liqueur, hot tea with lemon served in a glass, an overflowing plate of whipped creamy chocolate cakes, a plate of small round lace cookies, a tray of various chocolates.

By this time, we have all drunk quite a lot of *nalewka* and are pink-cheeked and amiable.

After *kolacje,* Danuta puts on a klezmer CD and turns up the volume. She says, "Klezmer is my favorite music!"

She sings and sweeps into the kitchen our empty plates in her arms.

Later, we gather on the couch. Jurek, Krzysztof's dad, lifts his guitar off its stand and plays for us, spot-on Led Zeppelin.

The next day, Krzysztof, Maria and I are out again exploring drizzly Lublin. We take refuge in a dark rambling café and order coffee, wrapping our hands around our cups for warmth. In her soft voice, Maria tells me of her aunt Maria, her namesake, whom she deeply admires. Her aunt helped a Jewish family during the war. The story does not end well. The family survives but does not stay connected with Maria, perhaps breaks promises, leaves a bitter taste. We look down into our cups.

The next morning over breakfast Krzysztof asks me,

"Are you feeling the responsibility of being the sole representative of the Jewish people?"

🍎
Helena in Warszawa

Helena is much more like me than Krzysztof, more possibly my parallel self. Right off we have much in common: our name, our age, our Jewishness, our queerness. Her parents survived the Nazis and returned to Warsaw after the war. She inherited the very Warsaw apartment she had grown up in. Helena is a public intellectual, an historian and sociologist.

One May evening Helena and her partner, Agata, invite me to their Warsaw home for Shabbos dinner. I bring a challah from the Charlotte Menora bakery and a bouquet of pink peonies.

Before our meal, Helena asks me to make *Kiddish*. I am moved by this, and sing slowly, full of the weight of singing *Kiddish* in Warsaw today when there is hardly a Jew left to recite it. We sit across the laden table and lean in, straining to understand each other. Helena's English is limited, my Polish comes in fits and starts. It is slow going, we're dancing a multilingual waltz, but if my parents had stayed in Poland after the war the way her parents had, we could have been friends from childhood.

Helena, I recognize your face, like a cousin. Your cheeks, your springy hair. Because you look familiar, do I assume too much? I feel hobbled that I can't speak with you more fully, that I can't go deeper with my questions or my understanding, that I can't tell you what it means to me to meet you.

Do I think we understand each other better than we do? The undercurrents between us run strong. We use a river of body language, tilts of head, nods and smiles, to get across what words don't.

I am afraid I am making you up. That's how strong is my desire to connect. I'd rather make you up than feel I don't understand. I want a translator but don't want anyone to dilute our contact. I want a translator of nuance, why did you just laugh? What did I miss? I want it all now, of course. It's been so long, this disconnect.

Back home, when political news from Poland is dire, I email Helena and Agata, reaching out a far-away hand. Helena replies, *we embrace and kiss you.*

༄

A June evening. I am sitting alone on the dock at Holny Lake, in the northeast corner of Poland, yards away from the border with Lithuania. The lake is glittering. It is just before Shabbos. Very, very quietly I begin to sing a Shabbos song. So quiet I do not ripple water or disturb birds in the trees.

None of this comes easy: constantly demanding of myself, be open, look past the surface for a way in, draw up the positive. I battle my own pessimism, my cellular, hormonal fear.

Sometimes the temptation to lie is overwhelming. Like a small darting animal, my mind scurries for a way out. These tender, nascent friendships. What do I want from them? What do I give?

Again and again, I push off into a new paradigm. Past war, past rupture, continuity.

There are other skaters on this ice. I keep meeting them, and they keep meeting me.

One foot on spring ice, 1 step forward.

"Now I Will You to Be a Bold Swimmer"

"Now I Will You to Be a Bold Swimmer"

For Abraham, Luc, India, Madeline, James, Charles

I pass to you, dear ones,
our people's mysteries.

You lay out your palms like cups
and I pour in the stuff of our story.

Many times I ask my blood
does it feed you

to carry our history
in its darkness and its radiance?

When is it better to remember?
When is it better to forget?

My blood says
you will spice the tale

with your own days and nights
and salt it with your living.

        Title from Walt Whitman, *Song of Myself*

Do Strangers Make Us Human?

My father left a few important facts, typed on a piece of white paper and folded in half. My mother refused to talk, though sometimes, when we sat together on the couch, she sat so close there was no space between her hip and mine. And Pani Mokska? Does anyone out there know?

(I'm here, I'm listening.)

Pani Mokska of Warszawa. You were a stranger to my parents and yet you risked your life to hide them. Because you were hungry and they gave you money for food? Because the pain of taking them in was less than the pain of turning them away?

(All was strange, so nothing was.)

Pani Mokska, why do I hear you now? Because I have been in Warszawa more than once, twice, three times? Because I can say the name of your neighborhood, Grochów, can point to it on a map?

I carry you like an ache, Pani Mokska. You gave my parents a cellar room in your house with a high window to your flower garden. I want to give you something, with as many petals as that.

(I'm dead. You don't owe me.)

What if I tell the story like my father did? I don't want you trapped, with your hand curled around the coin. I want to hear you tell the story. Why do I hear you now?

(You hear because you are getting closer.)

Alarming, the thin line between being and not being. A few breaths. It can end with a hand held firm over mouth and nose, and a baby's life is over. This act was carried out, I have read, in more than one hiding place.

My great-nephew is Luc. His name means light. He is new and small, dependent. He takes your kindness, unknowing and easy, like pulling a raspberry from the bush. I will tell him the story someday, how you gave sanctuary to his great-grandparents, on another continent, a hundred years before. Then he will make of this what he will, perhaps forget, perhaps remember when his child is born. Or not.

You had a daughter, Pani Mokska. Did your daughter have a child?

> *(In the rubble, we lost each other.)*

Maybe she is still alive, Pani Mokska. Maybe she remembers the two people hidden in the cellar, maybe she wonders.

> *(We never once sat together, your father, your mother
> and I, never once sat at my kitchen table.)*

What of you, Pani Mokska, did my parents bear? What church-deep creed lingered in your glance? And my parents, what did they regret? You were the thin cloth between them and death. Years later, in their dark bedroom, they whispered of you.

> *(He sang sometimes, your father. He sang to her.
> They were young and had each other. I envied them that.)*

Did you, Pani Mokska, ever look unmasked into my mother's eyes, my father's eyes? I want this. Why? Do I look the most revealing, most frightening of my truths in the face? Do I want you to do this instead of me? For me? Do I want you to finish off war for once and for all?

> *(Yes, you do.)*

Thin, afraid, maybe silent, maybe shaking in Warszawa dusk. Bombs falling, city crushed, three strangers, more alike than different. Was there a moment when you recognized each other?

> *(You think you know, but you don't.)*

Did you see beyond that day, down a line of oncoming souls? Did your God count these souls for you? Was it Sunday, were you gathering your gloves, checking your reflection in the mirror, when two strangers came out of shadow?

> *(Did I open the door?)*

Acknowledgments

With deep gratitude for my teachers who inspired and encouraged me, for the communities of women writers, publishers and readers who know the power of words and create space for this book to come into being, for my beloved and magnificent family and friends walking with me on this many-year, many-mile journey.

Grateful acknowledgment is made to the editors of the publications in which the following poems first appeared:

About Place Journal: "documents of flight"

basalt: "All That I Have Is a River"

Blue Mountain Review:
 "*Doina* in the Study House"
 "It Could Happen"
 "Field Lake Road" (haikus)

Cathexis Northwest Press:
 "Not Asking"
 "Speaking to the Dead"

Crack the Spine: "First Person Singular"

Evening Street Review: "Lichen"

Fourteen Hills: "Imagine the Snail"

Free State Review: "Everybody Knows"

Glint Literary Journal: "All By Myself"

Midwest Quarterly: "[Bala] From Kalisz, Air, Earth"

Porter House Review: "A Quarrel With the Village of My Birth"

Rattling Wall: "Que Sera, Sera"

The Cape Rock: "Necklace"

Travelers' Tales Solas Awards: *"Do Widzenia"*

TRIVIA: Voices of Feminism: "Snake I Come"

Visitant:
    "Playing Piano Between Wars"
    "Pleated Skirt" ["Tante Fela"]

Poem Index

A
A Quarrel With the Village of My Birth 9
All by myself 62
All That I Have Is a River 10

B
Bala from Kalisz, Air, Earth 14
Baltic Romance 39

D
Deliverance 46
Do Strangers Make Us Human? 76
Do Widzenia, 1 12
Do Widzenia, 2 29
Do Widzenia, 3 43
Do Widzenia, 4 50
Do Widzenia, 5 61
documents of flight 15
Doina in the Study House 31

E
Everybody Knows 25

F
First Person Singular 53

H
haiku, 1 each field has its blooms 28
haiku, 2 gray wind off the lake 47
haiku, 3 fringe the lake in reeds 58

haiku, 4 east sun on my cheek 65
Half-light 13

I

Imagine the Snail 32
In Krasnogruda the Cuckoo Wakes Me 48
In the Upstairs Bedroom 33
It Could Happen 40

K

Kitchen 54

L

Lichen 17
Like a Badger 19
Like One of Those 45

N

Names Go Traveling With No Valises 16
Native Speaker 44
Necklace 23
New Content 56
Not Asking 36
"Now I Will You to Be a Bold Swimmer" 75

P

Playing Piano Between Wars 18

Q

Que Sera, Sera 3

S

Snake I Come 26
Speaking to the Dead 24
Spring Ice 63

T

Tante Fela 52
The Scarecrow 30
The soft parts all rubbed away 51
Transgress 49
Travel to Szczebrzeszyn 41
Twaróg 34

W

W kuchni 55

Helena Lipstadt is the author of two chapbooks, *Leave Me Signs* and *If My Heart Were a Desert*. Her poems have been featured in *The Midwest Quarterly*, *Sinister Wisdom*, *About Place Journal,* and elsewhere. Anthologies that hold her prose include *The Challenge of Shalom* and *A Dangerous New World: Maine Voices on the Climate Crisis*.

Her work has been generously supported by residencies at WUJS Arts Project Arad, Israel and Borderland Foundation, Sejny, Poland.

She studied with poets Melanie Kaye/Kantrowitz, Irena Klepfisz, Laurel Ann Bogen and Terry Wolverton.

Lipstadt once accepted Bedouin hospitality in a tent on the shoulder of Mount Sinai, traveled up the Nile River in a felucca, and in Poland, helped re-create a 17th-century Polish synagogue. She also designed and built her home in Maine by hand.

She was born in Berlin and now lives in Los Angeles, California and Blue Hill, Maine.

www.ingramcontent.com/pod-product-compliance
Lightning Source LLC
Chambersburg PA
CBHW031124160426
43192CB00008B/1102